PETERSON'S
CARNIVORE DIET

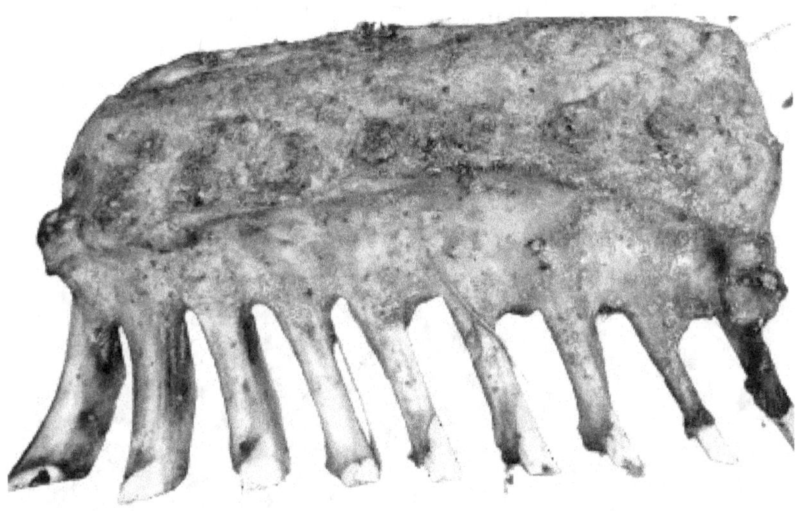

The ultimate No Carb Diet for a Healthier you

Everett Mike

Disclaimer

This book contains information sourced from reputable sources. While every effort has been made to ensure the accuracy and reliability of the information presented, the author and publisher cannot guarantee the validity of all materials or be held responsible for any consequences resulting from their use. Readers are encouraged to consult additional sources and exercise their own judgment when applying the information.

The information provided in this book is intended for educational and informational purposes only. The content should not be considered a substitute for professional medical advice, diagnosis, or treatment.

Table of Contents

Introduction

In a world where the advancements of contemporary medicine appear boundless in their ability to address our afflictions, certain individuals choose extraordinary paths, venturing forth in search of alternative routes to health and vitality. Among them is Mikhaila Peterson, a courageous woman who challenged the orthodox beliefs surrounding medical treatments and embarked on an awe-inspiring expedition towards achieving healing.

Mikhaila's tale is a testament to her unwavering strength, unwavering resolve, and an unyielding quest for solutions to her chronic health issues. Since her early years, she faced an array of physical and mental obstacles that appeared unconquerable. Before she even reached her 22nd birthday, she relied on more than 10 medications solely to cope with her diverse ailments.

Mikhaila's existence was clouded by a lengthy list of ailments. Bipolar disorder, hypersomnia, Lyme disease, psoriasis, and eczema plagued her daily life, casting a shadow of constant pain.

In addition to all this, Juvenile rheumatoid arthritis had taken a toll on her joints, leaving them ravaged. Since fifth grade, she relied on antidepressants to navigate through the challenging path ahead. It felt as though her own body had turned against her, and with each passing day, hope slipped further away.

Nevertheless, amidst her overwhelming desolation, a flicker of hope materialized. A momentous breakthrough unfolded as she eradicated gluten from her meals and witnessed a striking amelioration in her stubborn rash. This apparently trivial triumph ignited a profound sense of inquisitiveness within her. Could her dietary choices wield a more substantial influence on her path to recovery?

Motivated by an insatiable quest for knowledge and a desire for better health, Mikhaila ventured further into the realm of dietary interventions. She embarked on an exploration of the ketogenic diet, eagerly anticipating a potential remedy for her overwhelming symptoms. Despite encountering a combination of favorable and unfavorable outcomes, she remained unwavering in her determination. In her tireless pursuit, she unexpectedly came across an extraordinary tale about a woman who had successfully healed her Lyme disease by adopting an exclusively carnivorous diet consisting solely of meat.

Driven by desperation and fueled by unwavering determination, Mikhaila reached a pivotal moment in her life. She resolved to wholeheartedly adopt the strictest type of carnivore diet – Lion diet, renouncing all other food groups. Till today, this audacious choice garnered attention and skepticism from the medical community, but she disregarded their doubts. With everything to gain and nothing to lose, she embarked on this radical path.

After years of faithfully following the lion diet, she testified that all her symptoms have entered a state of remission. The change is nothing less than extraordinary. She has emerged from the depths of enduring illness into the radiance of robust well-being.

After seeing the remarkable results of the lion diet on his daughter, Jordan Peterson decided to give it a chance. During an appearance on the renowned Joe Rogan podcast, Peterson enthusiastically shared his experience, stating, "I've shed 50 pounds since adopting this lion diet. My appetite has diminished by about 70%, and I no longer experience blood sugar dysregulation issues. Surprisingly, I require significantly less sleep." In addition, he confidently asserted that his anxiety and depression had vanished, and he felt remarkably mentally alert. Peterson concluded, "And you won't believe it, but even my gum disease has miraculously disappeared. It's truly astonishing!"

The story of human evolution has been a captivating voyage spanning nearly 2 million years. Our ancient ancestors, known as cavemen, were formidable apex predators with a strong preference for meat. They roamed the Earth as skilled hunters, relying on the meat of large animals to sustain and thrive. This hyper-carnivorous diet provided them with an abundance of protein, healthy fats, and limited carbohydrates, perfectly aligned with our human design and efficiently meeting their nutritional needs.

During those times, the fruits, nuts, and vegetables we know today were virtually non-existent. It wasn't until around 7,000 years ago, coinciding with the rise of agriculture, that grains made their appearance.

The transition from hunting and gathering to agriculture marked a significant turning point in human history. As societies started cultivating crops and domesticating animals, the human diet underwent a drastic transformation. Grains such as wheat, rice, and corn became staple food sources, leading to a shift towards a carbohydrate-rich diet which also introduced several health implications.

The introduction of grains and the subsequent shift towards a diet centered around carbohydrates had profound consequences for human health. Our bodies faced challenges in processing and metabolizing the increased intake of grains and other refined carbohydrates as we adapted to this new dietary landscape. The excessive consumption of these foods, combined with a sedentary lifestyle, contributed to the rise of civilization diseases such as diabetes and heart disease.

Reflecting on Peterson's stories and the impact of dietary changes on human health, it becomes clear that returning to our ancestral roots may hold the key to improved well-being. Traditional civilizations unaffected by the modern industrialized food system offer valuable insights into the benefits of consuming whole, unprocessed foods.

Within the pages of this book, we will explore the science behind the lion diet and its potential to revolutionize our understanding of human nutrition. Prepare to challenge your preconceived notions, for this tale is one of courage, hope, and the extraordinary power of the lion diet to transform life.

<u>**Writer's Check-In**</u>: *Is Inflammation Controlling Your Life?*

Let's do a quick health check. Answer these questions honestly:

- Do you often feel tired, even after a full night's sleep?

- Do you experience frequent bloating, digestive issues, or unexplained weight gain?

- Do your joints ache, even when you haven't exercised?

- Do you get headaches, brain fog, or find it hard to concentrate?

- Do you have high blood sugar, high cholesterol, or trouble managing stress?

- Have you been diagnosed with an inflammatory condition like arthritis, diabetes, or heart disease?

If you answer yes to two or more of these questions, your body may be battling chronic inflammation—and it's time to take control.

But don't worry, you're not alone. In the next chapters, we'll dive into exactly why this is happening and, more importantly, what you can do to reverse it.

<u>Other Book(s) by the Author</u>

Carnivore Diet on a Budget

Link: rb.gy/x2577f QR

Lion Diet, why does it work?

The Lion Diet is more than just an elimination diet—it's a powerful tool for resetting your body by tackling inflammation and healing your gut. To truly understand why this diet is effective, you need to grasp how inflammation and gut health are deeply connected.

The Gut Health: The Microbiome in our Gut

When you are dragging yourself out of bed, feeling sluggish, dealing with brain fog, and constantly battling food reactions you can't quite pinpoint. The problem is probably coming from your gut.

Inside you, trillions of bacteria are working day and night, forming what's called your **gut microbiome**. This ecosystem isn't just about digestion—it's the command center of your immune system, mood, and overall health. When balanced, it strengthens your immunity, reduces inflammation, and keeps your energy levels stable. But when disrupted? It can lead to chronic fatigue, autoimmune reactions, and digestive struggles.

Think of it as a bustling city with different microbial species performing specialized jobs. Some bacteria help break down food and extract essential nutrients, while others produce compounds that regulate immune responses and even influence brain function.

When your microbiome is balanced, it acts as a shield, keeping harmful pathogens in check, reducing inflammation, and ensuring your body functions optimally. It aids in nutrient absorption, produces vitamins like B12 and K2, and maintains the integrity of the gut lining. A thriving microbiome supports mental clarity, stabilizes mood, and keeps your energy levels steady throughout the day. This happens when you eat the right food.

As an example, when you eat a diet rich in fiber from foods like lentils, apples, and asparagus. These fiber-rich foods serve as prebiotics, feeding beneficial gut bacteria such as *Bifidobacteria* and *Lactobacillus*. As these bacteria flourish, they produce short-chain fatty acids (SCFAs) like butyrate, which help reduce gut inflammation and strengthen the intestinal lining. This, in turn, prevents harmful bacteria like *Clostridium difficile* from overgrowing and causing digestive issues. Additionally, the gut produces neurotransmitters like serotonin, contributing to improved mood and mental clarity. As a result, you experience fewer energy crashes, better digestion, and a stronger immune response. While the lion diet lacks fiber, nutrient-dense animal foods like bone broth and organ meats can help maintain gut health by supporting the gut lining and reducing inflammation. Also, by removing plant toxins, and processed foods, it reduces gut inflammation, starves bad bacteria, and allows beneficial bacteria to thrive.

A negative example of this is when you consume a diet high in processed foods, refined sugars, and artificial additives. These foods can feed harmful bacteria like *Clostridium perfringens* and *Escherichia coli*, leading to an imbalance in the gut microbiome (dysbiosis). As these harmful bacteria overgrow, they produce toxins that damage the gut lining, causing increased intestinal permeability, commonly known as "leaky gut." This allows undigested food particles and toxins to enter the bloodstream, triggering widespread inflammation. The result can be digestive issues like bloating, diarrhea, or constipation, as well as systemic effects such as brain fog, fatigue, mood swings, and even an increased risk of autoimmune diseases.

Leaky gut isn't something that happens overnight. It builds up over years of consuming inflammatory foods like grains, dairy, processed sugars, and seed oils. Stress, medications, and even environmental toxins further damage the gut lining, making it more vulnerable. When your gut is compromised, food sensitivities skyrocket. You might develop an autoimmune condition. Your body isn't betraying you; it's trying to protect itself. The modern diet—filled with processed foods, sugars, and artificial additives—has wreaked havoc on our gut health. These foods fuel harmful bacteria, weaken gut barriers, and set the stage for inflammation.

MORE! MORE!! MORE!!!

Want our previous book on the lion diet with 30 meal plans? Want our free journal recipes?

Visit: bit.ly/4bbvU5R

Inflammation: The Silent Trigger You Need to Understand

Let's talk about something that's happening inside your body right now—inflammation. You may not see it, but trust me, it's either working to protect you or slowly wearing you down.

Inflammation is your body's built-in defense system. When faced with harmful invaders like bacteria, damaged cells, or toxins, your immune system jumps into action, triggering inflammation to fight back and begin the healing process. Sounds great, right? Well, not always.

There are two types of inflammation—one is helpful, the other… not so much.

- Acute Inflammation is your body's first line of defense. Think of what happens when you cut your finger, it turns red, swells, and might feel warm. That's your immune system rushing to repair the damage. It's short-lived and essential for healing.

- Chronic Inflammation, however, is a different story. This is when your body stays in fight mode even when there's no clear enemy. Instead of healing, it starts attacking healthy tissues, leading to long-term damage. This kind of inflammation plays a major role in conditions like diabetes, heart disease, and even obesity.

The big question is: What impact does Chronic Inflammation have on your health?

Chronic inflammation is like a fire that never fully burns out—it smolders beneath the surface, slowly causing damage without you even realizing it. Unlike acute inflammation, which helps you heal, chronic inflammation does the opposite. It keeps your immune system in a constant state of alert, even when there's no real threat. And over time, this takes a serious toll on your body.

So, why should you care? Because chronic inflammation has been directly linked to some of the most serious health conditions. The persistent inflammatory state can damage tissues and organs, leading to significant health complications such as heart disease, diabetes, cancer, arthritis, and digestive disorders like Crohn's disease and ulcerative colitis. Instead of protecting you, your immune system begins attacking your own healthy tissues, leading to pain, organ damage, and long-term health problems.

How can Chronic Inflammation Slowly Destroys Your Health

Chronic inflammation is at the root of nearly every major disease, many of which may already be affecting you or someone you love. Let's break it down:

1. Heart Disease: The Silent Artery Killer

Inflammation plays a key role in atherosclerosis, the dangerous buildup of plaques in your arteries. These plaques aren't just harmless blockages—they become unstable when inflammatory cells attack them, increasing the risk of a heart attack or stroke. Over time, inflammation weakens blood vessels, making cardiovascular problems more likely.

2. Metabolic Disorders: The Link Between Inflammation, Diabetes, and Obesity

Did you know inflammation could stop your body from using insulin properly? Insulin resistance, a major driver of type 2 diabetes, happens when chronic inflammation interferes with insulin's ability to regulate blood sugar.

Additionally, carrying excess visceral fat (fat around your organs) fuels inflammation, creating a vicious cycle that leads to obesity and metabolic dysfunction.

3. Cancer: Fueling Uncontrolled Cell Growth

Chronic inflammation can damage your DNA, promote rapid cell division, and even block your body's natural ability to remove faulty cells. This creates the perfect conditions for cancer to develop and spread. Long-term inflammation has been linked to cancers of the liver, colon, stomach, and more.

4. Autoimmune Diseases: When Your Body Attacks Itself

In conditions like rheumatoid arthritis, lupus, and inflammatory bowel disease (IBD), chronic inflammation causes the immune system to turn against its own tissues. This leads to ongoing pain, swelling, and organ damage. Without proper management, autoimmune diseases can lead to lifelong disability.

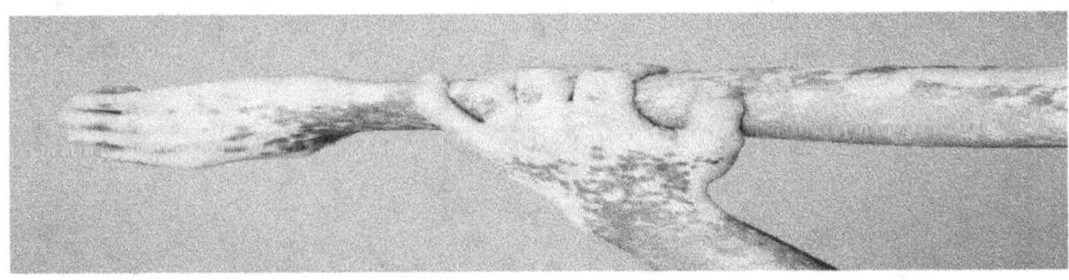

5. Brain Health: The Hidden Trigger Behind Alzheimer's and Parkinson's

Scientists are discovering that chronic inflammation doesn't just affect your body—it can damage your brain too. Overactive immune cells in the brain contribute to Alzheimer's, Parkinson's, and other neurodegenerative diseases, leading to memory loss, cognitive decline, and nervous system disorders.

6. Respiratory Issues: When Inflammation Steals Your Breath

If you struggle with asthma or chronic obstructive pulmonary disease (COPD), inflammation may be the reason behind your breathing difficulties. It causes airway swelling, excess mucus production, and hypersensitivity, making it harder to breathe and leaving your lungs vulnerable to long-term damage.

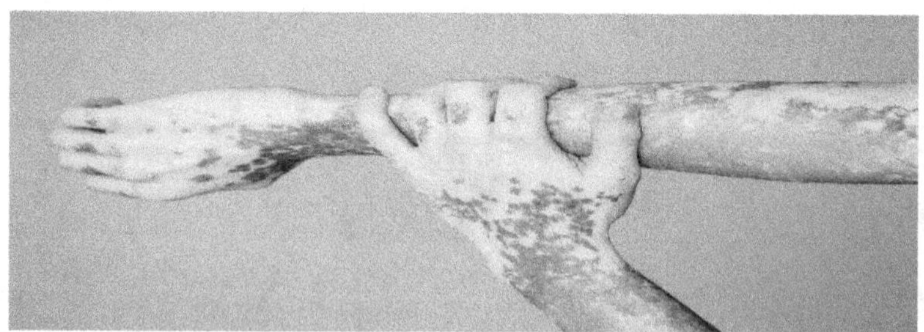

Your body is like a finely tuned orchestra, where sleep, diet, exercise, and stress management each play a critical role in creating harmony. When one is out of balance, the entire system suffers. These four pillars don't just support your well-being, they shape the very foundation of your health.

Sleep isn't just about rest; it's when your body repairs itself, strengthens the immune system, and reduces inflammation. Without quality sleep, even the healthiest diet or exercise routine won't be enough to counteract damage.

Exercise keeps your blood circulating, muscles strong, and metabolism in check. It's also one of the most effective ways to reduce chronic inflammation, lower insulin resistance, and keep your heart healthy.

Stress management is often overlooked but plays a powerful role in disease prevention. Chronic stress disrupts hormone levels, weakens immunity, and fuels inflammation—silently working against your health.

Yet, while all these factors matter, one stands out as the most immediate and impactful in this book: diet. Lion Diet.

The food you eat isn't just fuel; it's information for your body. Every bite has the power to either heal or harm, to fight inflammation or ignite it

When you eat unhealthy foods, you might develop a leaky gut, when you develop a leaky gut, it will cause inflammation which can result in any chronic disease.

"Let Your Food Be Your Medicine, and Your Medicine be Your Food"

Hippocrates

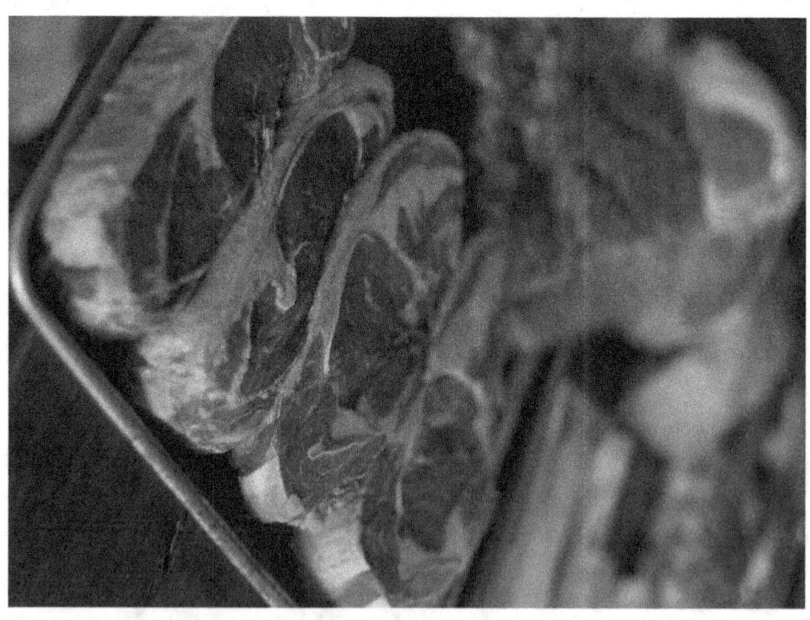

Your diet is one of the most powerful tools you have to control or fuel inflammation. Every meal you eat either supports your body's natural healing processes or triggers harmful inflammatory responses. But how exactly does this happen? Let's break down the key mechanisms behind diet-induced inflammation:

Oxidative Stress – Think of oxidative stress as internal "rust." When there's an imbalance between free radicals (harmful molecules) and antioxidants (protective compounds), your cells become damaged. Diets high in processed foods, fried foods, and artificial additives flood your body with free radicals while depriving you of the antioxidants needed to neutralize them. Over time, this damage leads to chronic inflammation and accelerates aging and disease.

Gut Microbiota Imbalance – Your gut isn't just responsible for digestion; it's also a key regulator of inflammation. A diet high in refined carbs, sugars, and processed foods disrupts the balance of gut bacteria, allowing harmful microbes to thrive. This imbalance weakens your intestinal barrier, allowing toxins and inflammatory compounds to leak into your bloodstream—a process known as leaky gut syndrome—which fuels widespread inflammation.

Insulin Resistance – When you eat too many sugary and refined carbohydrate-rich foods, your body has to release more insulin to keep blood sugar levels in check. But over time, your cells become desensitized to insulin, leading to insulin resistance. This condition doesn't just set the stage for type 2 diabetes—it also triggers inflammation, as excess insulin promotes the release of inflammatory cytokines, harming blood vessels and organs.

How the Lion Diet Heals

The Lion Diet is an extreme elimination diet consisting solely of ruminant meat (like beef and lamb), salt, and water. While it may sound restrictive, its simplicity is what makes it a powerful tool for healing leaky guts and reducing chronic inflammation. Here's how:

1. Eliminates Gut Irritants

Many common foods, especially grains, dairy, legumes, processed foods, and seed oil can trigger gut inflammation and worsen leaky gut syndrome. These foods contain lectins, gluten, oxalates, and other antinutrients that can irritate the gut lining. The Lion Diet removes all potential irritants, giving the gut a chance to heal.

2. Restores Gut Barrier Function

Leaky gut occurs when the intestinal lining becomes compromised, allowing toxins, undigested food particles, and bacteria to enter the bloodstream, triggering widespread inflammation. The Lion Diet is rich in collagen, amino acids (like glutamine), and healthy fats, which help repair the gut lining and restore tight junctions in the intestines, preventing further leakage.

3. Reduces Chronic Inflammation

By removing inflammatory foods, the body experiences a natural reset. Since processed foods, sugar, and seed oils are primary drivers of inflammation, their absence allows inflammatory markers to drop. Additionally, ruminant meat contains omega-3 fatty acids and conjugated linoleic acid (CLA), both of which have anti-inflammatory properties.

4. Supports Balanced Immune Response

When the gut is inflamed, the immune system stays on high alert, often leading to autoimmune reactions and chronic disease. Because the Lion Diet eliminates common immune triggers, it can help calm an overactive immune system, reducing symptoms of autoimmune conditions like rheumatoid arthritis, Crohn's disease, and eczema.

5. Promotes Metabolic Health and Insulin Sensitivity

Since insulin resistance and blood sugar fluctuations contribute to inflammation, a diet free from refined carbs and sugars naturally improves insulin sensitivity. By stabilizing blood sugar levels, the Lion Diet prevents spikes in inflammatory cytokines, further reducing inflammation and promoting metabolic balance.

The Lion Diet acts as a "reset button" for the body, eliminating inflammatory triggers, healing the gut lining, and restoring balance to the immune system. While it may not be necessary for everyone long-term, many people find that using it as a temporary gut-healing protocol helps them identify food sensitivities, reverse inflammation, and regain control over their health.

Would you consider trying a strict but healing elimination diet like the Lion Diet to test its effects on your health.

The takeaway is that your gut health is the foundation of your well-being. If you're constantly dealing with fatigue, bloating, or autoimmune flare-ups, it's time to focus on healing from the inside out. The Lion Diet isn't just another fad—it's a return to the way our bodies were meant to function.

We've Sold Over 500 Copies—But Need Your Help!

While over 500 copies have been sold, only 8 readers have left a rating, and 2 negative reviews have hurt the book's credibility and visibility. These buyers though it to be written by Jordan or Mikhaila Peterson, despite our clear disclaimer.

If you find value in this book, please take a minute to leave a review or rating. Your support helps others discover it and means a lot to the author. Just use the link or QR code—thank you!

If you enjoy the book, please consider leaving a review through this link.   - https://rb.gy/dmuolm or

by scanning this QR code:

Part II: Discovering the Lion Diet

Rethinking Nutrition: Against the Demonization of Meat

The search for the "best" diet is a journey, not a one-size-fits-all answer. Your body is unique, shaped by genetics, lifestyle, health conditions, and personal preferences. What fuels one person's vitality might not work the same for another. Instead of chasing a universal solution, the key is to listen to your body and tailor your nutrition to what truly supports your well-being. This means factoring in your metabolic health, food sensitivities, daily routine, and even cultural traditions to create a sustainable way of eating.

That's exactly what the Lion Diet offers—a simple, meat-only approach designed to eliminate food triggers and reset your system. For decades, meat has been unfairly blamed for health issues, pushing many to avoid it altogether. But is meat really the villain, or have we misunderstood its role? In this chapter, we'll challenge common misconceptions, dive into our ancestral connection with meat, and explore why it might be the missing piece in your journey to optimal health.

Perspective on History and Meat Consumption

For most of human history, long before the agricultural revolution, our ancestors thrived as hunters, gatherers, and fishers. Their diets revolved around wild games, fish, and naturally foraged foods—without the processed sugars and refined carbohydrates that dominate modern eating habits. What's fascinating is that chronic illnesses like high blood pressure, cardiovascular disease, and obesity were virtually nonexistent in these populations. So, if meat was a staple in their diet, why isn't it the culprit behind today's health epidemics?

Meat and the Strength of Ancient Generations

Take the Mongols, for example one of history's most powerful civilizations. Their empire was built on strength, endurance, and a diet centered around animal-based nutrition. They thrived on meat, animal fat, and fermented dairy, rarely consuming grains or plant-based foods. This high-energy diet fueled their legendary warriors, allowing them to ride for days with minimal food and still maintain peak physical performance.

Beyond the Mongols, modern-day forager societies like the Tsimane, the Hadza, and the Arctic Inuit provide living proof that a diet rich in animal protein supports longevity and resilience. These groups experience lower rates of lifestyle-related diseases, showing that their nutrient-dense, meat-based diets are closely aligned with what our bodies evolved to consume. As paleoanthropologist Peter Ungar explains, "There is a clear discordance between what we eat today and what our ancestors evolved to eat."

What if the real problem isn't meat itself but the way we've altered our diets in modern times? This perspective encourages us to rethink our relationship with meat, not as the enemy, but as an ancestral superfood that has fueled human evolution for centuries. It supports the idea that our bodies are well-adapted to diets rich in animal protein and fats.

Emergence of Agriculture and Disease

Having established from our ancient history that meat is not the problem, we can examine something else which is agriculture.

The shift from foraging to farming brought about a dramatic change in human diets. The introduction of grains and an over-reliance on carbohydrate-rich crops coincided with new patterns of disease and nutritional deficiencies. It wasn't until after agriculture became widespread that many chronic illnesses and metabolic disorders began to appear. This historical context challenges the modern narrative that eating animal products is inherently unhealthy.

While plants offer some essential nutrients, some contain natural defense chemicals that can contribute to health issues in sensitive individuals. Here are a few examples:

1. Gluten-Containing Grains (Wheat, Barley, Rye) – Linked to celiac disease and gluten sensitivity, causing digestive distress, inflammation, and autoimmune reactions.

2. Legumes (Soy, Peanuts, Lentils, Beans) – Contain lectins and phytic acid, which can interfere with

nutrient absorption and may contribute to gut irritation and autoimmune issues.

3. Nightshades (Tomatoes, Potatoes, Eggplants, Peppers) – Contain alkaloids like solanine, which have been associated with joint pain, inflammation, and digestive issues in some people.

4. Oxalate-Rich Plants (Spinach, Almonds, Beets, Rhubarb) – High oxalate intake has been linked to kidney stones and calcium absorption issues.

5. Industrial Seed Oils (Soybean, Canola, Corn Oil) – Highly processed and rich in omega-6 fatty acids, which promote chronic inflammation and metabolic disorders when consumed in excess.

While some people tolerate these plants well, others experience significant health improvements by reducing or eliminating them.

Revaluating Modern Perceptions

The narrative that meat consumption is intrinsically harmful is a relatively recent development, emerging prominently with the advent of agriculture and the modern food industry. Historical evidence and anthropological studies suggest that:

- **Human Evolution:** For the majority of our evolution, meat was a significant component of the human diet, contributing essential proteins, fats, vitamins, and minerals.

- **Disease Patterns:** Many contemporary chronic diseases are linked to dietary shifts post-agriculture—specifically, increased consumption of processed foods, refined sugars, and a departure from nutrient-dense, whole foods.

- **Adaptation:** Humans are not "trapped in Stone Age bodies in a fast-food world." Instead, our physiology may be better suited to diets that more closely resemble those of our hunter-gatherer ancestors.

The historical and anthropological record challenges the modern demonization of meat. Whether it's the foraging lifestyles of the Tsimane, Hadza, and Inuit or the robust warrior diets of the Mongols, there is compelling evidence that meat has been a fundamental and health-sustaining part of the human diet for millennia. As we reassess our nutritional choices today, understanding these historical contexts can provide valuable insight into what our bodies may be best adapted to—and why a return to simpler, more ancestral dietary patterns might hold promise for modern health challenges.

Understanding the Rationale Behind a Meat-Only Diet

The meat-only diet, often referred to as the carnivore diet or Lion Diet, involves consuming exclusively animal products, primarily meat, and excluding all plant-based foods. There are various suggested reasons for its potential benefits:

1. **Evolutionary Perspective:** Our ancestors thrived on animal-based diets long before agriculture introduced grains and processed foods. Returning to such a diet aligns with our evolutionary biology and may promote better health.

2. **Elimination of Antinutrients:** Certain plant compounds, known as antinutrients (e.g., lectins,

oxalates, phytates), can interfere with nutrient absorption or trigger sensitivities in some individuals. By excluding plant foods, a meat-only diet eliminates these compounds, potentially reducing digestive discomfort and inflammation.

3. **Autoimmune and Inflammatory Conditions:** Some individuals report improvements in autoimmune and inflammatory conditions when adopting a carnivore diet. The hypothesis is that removing potential dietary triggers found in plant foods may alleviate symptoms.

4. **Nutrient Density:** Animal products, especially organ meats, are rich in essential nutrients such as vitamins B12, D, K2, iron, zinc, and omega-3 fatty acids. A well-planned meat-only diet can provide all necessary nutrients for health.

5. **Simplicity and Satiety:** Focusing solely on meat can simplify meal planning and may enhance satiety due to the high protein and fat content, potentially aiding in weight management.

The Science of Simplicity

Simplifying one's diet by focusing on whole, unprocessed foods can offer several benefits:

1. **Improved Digestion**: A diet centered around simple, whole foods can be easier to digest, reducing the burden on the digestive system and potentially alleviating issues like bloating and indigestion.

2. **Enhanced Nutrient Absorption:** Minimizing processed foods and additives may improve the body's ability to absorb and utilize nutrients effectively.

3. **Reduced Decision Fatigue:** Simplifying dietary choices can decrease the mental load associated with meal planning and decision-making, leading to a more sustainable eating pattern.

4. **Mindful Eating:** A minimalist approach to diet encourages mindfulness, allowing individuals to develop a greater appreciation for their food and its origins.

5. **Potential Weight Management:** Simpler diets often lead to reduced calorie intake and better portion control, which can be beneficial for weight management.

It's important to note that while some individuals report benefits from a meat-only diet, scientific research on its long-term health effects is limited. As with any dietary approach, it's advisable to consult with healthcare professionals before making significant changes to ensure nutritional adequacy and overall health.

Part 3: The Lion Diet Explained

Lion Diet

The Lion Diet is an extreme elimination diet that consists exclusively of ruminant meat, salt, and water. It is designed to identify and remove potential dietary irritants and triggers.

Key Components:

- Ruminant Meat: The diet includes meat from ruminant animals such as cows, sheep, and goats.

- Salt: Used to enhance flavor and maintain electrolyte balance.

- Water: The sole beverage permitted.

Exclusions:

The Lion Diet excludes all other foods and beverages, including:

- Non-ruminant meats (e.g., poultry, pork, fish)

- Dairy products

- Eggs

- Plant-based foods (fruits, vegetables, grains, legumes)

- Processed foods

- Additives and seasonings (other than salt)

By eliminating all potential dietary triggers, The Lion Diet offers a powerful way to pinpoint food intolerances and reset your system. It's not for the faint of heart, but for those seeking clarity in their diet, it could be a game-changer.

Why Ruminant Animals?

Ruminant meat is the gold standard in Lion Diet nutrition for a reason. It's nutrient-dense, anti-inflammatory, easy to digest, and provides steady energy, making it an optimal choice for those seeking a clean and healing diet.

What makes ruminants special is that unlike other animals, ruminants—such as cows, sheep, and goats—have a unique multi-chambered stomach that allows them to efficiently break down plant material. This process reduces anti-nutrients in their meat, making it more bioavailable and less likely to cause inflammation or digestive issues.

Simply put, ruminant meat delivers pure, high-quality nourishment without the common drawbacks of other protein sources. That's why it's the foundation of the Lion Diet.

How Much Should You Eat on the Lion Diet?

On the **Lion Diet**, there are no strict portion sizes or calorie counting. Instead, the goal is to **eat intuitively**—consuming as much as your body needs to feel satisfied. However, here are some guidelines to help you get started:

1. Eat Until You're Full, Not Stuffed

Since ruminant meat is nutrient-dense, you might feel satisfied with less food than you expect. Listen to your hunger signals and eat until you feel comfortably full, not overly stuffed.

2. General Daily Intake Guidelines

While everyone's needs vary, a common range for most people is:

- **Men:** 2–4 lbs (900g–1.8kg) of meat per day

- **Women:** 1.5–3 lbs (680g–1.4kg) of meat per day

Athletes or highly active individuals may require more.

3. Meal Frequency: 1-3 Meals Per Day

- **One Meal a Day (OMAD):** Some people find they naturally eat once per day due to the high satiety of meat.

- **Two Meals a Day (TMAD):** Many prefer splitting their intake into lunch and dinner for better digestion.

- **Three Meals a Day:** If you feel hungry more often, eating three meals is perfectly fine.

4. Prioritize Fatty Cuts

Since fat is your primary energy source on the Lion Diet, opt for fattier cuts like:

- Ribeye
- Ground beef (80/20 or 70/30)
- Lamb
- Brisket

Leaner meat may leave you feeling fatigued or hungry, so don't shy away from fat.

5. Listen to Your Body

Your appetite may fluctuate from day to day—this is normal. Some days you'll eat more, and some days less. Trust your body's signals rather than forcing a specific amount.

Why Do You Need Salt?

Salt isn't just a seasoning, it's an essential electrolyte that keeps your body functioning properly, especially on a lion diet. Since this diet naturally lacks many electrolyte-rich foods, adding salt to your water is crucial for preventing imbalances and staying energized. Here's why:

1. Prevents Electrolyte Imbalance

Cutting out carbs lowers insulin levels, which signals your kidneys flush out more sodium and water. This can lead to:

- Fatigue & dizziness

- Headaches

- Muscle cramps

- Heart palpitations (a sign of low electrolytes)

Drinking saltwater helps restore sodium levels and keeps your electrolytes balanced.

2. Fights Off the "Keto Flu"

Many people experience weaknesses, brain fog, and dehydration when transitioning to a carnivore diet. This happens due to rapid water loss. Adding salt to your water helps replenish lost minerals and prevents these uncomfortable symptoms.

3. Supports Hydration & Energy

Without carbs, your body holds on to less water, increasing the risk of dehydration. Salt helps you:

✓ Stay properly hydrated

✓ Boost energy levels

✓ Improve mental clarity

4. Digestion & Stomach Acid Production

Salt is essential for stomach acid production, which is key for digesting meat efficiently. If you struggle with bloating or indigestion, salt can help enhance your digestive function.

5. Prevents Muscle Cramps & Weakness

Low sodium levels can lead to tight muscles, cramping, and weakness. If you're experiencing leg cramps, increasing both salt and potassium can provide relief.

How to Take Salt Water on a lion Diet

Simple Electrolyte Drink:

- ½ to 1 tsp of sea salt (or Himalayan salt)

- 1 liter of water

- Optional: Add potassium & magnesium for extra balance

When to Drink It?

→ Morning: Start your day hydrated

→ Before or after workouts: Support performance & recovery

→ Whenever you feel lightheaded or fatigued

By making salt a staple in your carnivore diet, you'll avoid energy crashes, stay hydrated, and keep your body functioning at its best!

The Lion Diet is a highly restrictive eating plan that consists solely of ruminant meat (such as beef, lamb, and goat), salt, and water. This diet is designed as an elimination protocol to identify and remove potential dietary triggers, particularly for individuals with autoimmune or inflammatory conditions.

In contrast, other diets vary in their inclusivity and restrictions:

- **Carnivore Diet:** This diet includes all animal products, such as meat, fish, poultry, eggs, and some people add dairy and a few plants. It normally should exclude all plant-based foods but allows for a broader range of animal-derived nutrients compared to the Lion Diet.

- **Paleo Diet:** The Paleo Diet focuses on consuming whole, unprocessed foods that were presumably available to our Paleolithic ancestors. This includes meats, fish, fruits, vegetables, nuts, and seeds, while excluding processed foods, grains, legumes, and dairy. Unlike the Lion and Carnivore diets, the Paleo Diet incorporates a variety of plant-based foods.

The primary distinctions between the Lion Diet and many other diets are the level of restriction and the variety of foods allowed. The Lion Diet is the most restrictive, permitting only specific types of meat, salt, and water, aiming to eliminate all potential dietary variables. The Carnivore Diet, while still excluding plant-based foods, offers a wider selection of animal products. The Paleo Diet is the least restrictive among them, allowing a diverse range of both animal and plant-based foods.

Who Might Benefit from the Lion Diet?

1. **People with Autoimmune Disorders**

   - Individuals suffering from conditions like rheumatoid arthritis, lupus, multiple sclerosis, or Crohn's disease may find symptom relief by eliminating potential dietary triggers.

2. **Those with Severe Food Intolerances or Allergies**

   o People who react negatively to a wide range of foods, including dairy, grains, and plant-based foods, may benefit from the simplicity of the Lion Diet.

3. **Individuals with Chronic Inflammation or Gut Issues**

   o Conditions like leaky gut syndrome, IBS, and other digestive disorders may improve due to the highly digestible nature of ruminant meat and the absence of common irritants.

4. **People with Mental Health Struggles**

   o Some individuals with anxiety, depression, or even neurological disorders have reported improvements, possibly due to the diet's anti-inflammatory effects and nutrient density.

5. **Those Who Have Tried Other Elimination Diets Without Success**

o If diets like keto, paleo, or the standard carnivore diet (which includes eggs and dairy) have not provided relief, the Lion Diet offers a stricter approach.

Who Should Avoid the Lion Diet?

- **Pregnant or breastfeeding women** (due to its extreme restrictiveness).

- **Athletes or highly active individuals** may require more carbohydrates for energy.

- **People with a history of eating disorders** (as the extreme restriction may trigger unhealthy behaviors).

- **Anyone without a clear medical need** is not intended as a long-term, general health diet.

Since the diet is highly restrictive, those considering it should consult an open minded healthcare professional before making drastic dietary changes.

Combining the Lion Diet with Fasting: Maximizing Health Benefits.

The Lion Diet and fasting share a common principle, eliminating dietary triggers and allowing the body to heal. When used together, they can enhance metabolic flexibility, reduce inflammation, and improve digestion. However, careful implementation is necessary to prevent energy crashes or nutrient deficiencies.

Why Fasting Works Well with the Lion Diet

Since the Lion Diet consists of nutrient-dense ruminant meat, salt, and water, it naturally supports fasting by keeping blood sugar stable and providing long-lasting satiety. Fasting, in turn, enhances the benefits of the Lion Diet by:

- **Boosting Autophagy** – Helps remove damaged cells and toxins from the body.

- **Enhancing Gut Rest & Repair** – Allows the digestive system to heal, reducing bloating and sensitivities.

- **Improving Insulin Sensitivity** – Reduces blood sugar fluctuations, making energy levels more stable.

- **Supporting Mental Clarity** – Many people report reduced brain fog and improved focus.

Choosing the Right Fasting Method

Different fasting strategies work well with the Lion Diet depending on your experience level and goals.

A. Intermittent Fasting (16:8, 18:6, 20:4)

- Eat within a specific window (e.g., 8-hour, 6-hour, or 4-hour eating period).

- Ideal for beginners, allowing the body to gradually adjust to fasting.

- Works well with two large meals of ruminant meat per day.

B. One Meal a Day (OMAD)

- Eating one nutrient-dense meal within a 1–2 hour window.

- Effective for weight loss and metabolic healing but may be difficult at first.

- Ensure the meal is high in fat and protein to sustain energy.

C. Extended Fasting (24–72 Hours)

- Done occasionally for deeper autophagy and gut healing.

- Best for those already adapted to fasting and the Lion Diet.

- Hydration is crucial—drink salted water or bone broth to maintain electrolytes.

The Lion Diet is simple in its food choices but can become challenging when it comes to cost and sustainability. With careful planning, you can make this diet more budget-friendly while ensuring you get enough nutrients and variety.

1. Smart Sourcing: Finding Affordable Ruminant Meat

- Buy in Bulk – Purchasing large quantities of beef, lamb, or goat from a butcher or local farm often lowers the price per pound. Consider buying half or a quarter of a cow.

- Look for Discounts – Grocery stores often discount meat that's close to its sell-by date. Stock up and freeze for later.

- Shop at Local Farms & Butcher Shops – They may offer better deals than supermarkets, especially on grass-fed options.

- Explore Online Meat Suppliers – Some companies offer subscription boxes with discounts for bulk orders.

2. Meal Planning for Variety & Cost Savings

- Plan Weekly Meals – Instead of randomly buying meat, create a meal schedule with different cuts to ensure variety and nutrient balance.

- Rotate Meat Cuts – Mixing cheaper cuts (like ground beef or shank) with premium cuts (like ribeye) saves money.

- Utilize Bone Broth – Simmer bones for added minerals and hydration, reducing the need for supplements.

- Batch Cooking – Prepare meals in advance to save time and reduce the temptation of convenience foods.

3. Cooking Methods That Maximize Nutrition & Flavor

- Slow Cooking & Braising – Helps break down tougher, cheaper cuts, making them tender and more digestible.

- Grilling & Roasting – Simple, quick methods that retain flavor without unnecessary additives.

- Avoid Wasting Fat – Instead of discarding trimmed fat, render it into tallow for cooking.

4. Long-Term Affordability & Adaptation

- Reassess Budget Regularly – Adjust your meal plan based on seasonal meat prices and availability.

- Consider Rearing Your Own Meat (Long-Term) – If feasible, raising your own ruminant animals could be a cost-effective and sustainable option.

- Gradual Reintroduction (If Needed) – Once symptoms improve, consider reintroducing other low-inflammatory foods to expand options while maintaining the diet's benefits

Practical Guidance for Adopting the Lion Diet

Starting the Lion Diet can feel overwhelming at first, but with the right approach, it becomes second nature. Here's what has worked for many who have tried it:

1. Get Clear on What You Can Eat

The simplicity of this diet is both its strength and its challenge. You're only eating ruminant meats (beef, lamb, goat), salt, and water, nothing else. That means no sneaky seasonings, no sauces, and no coffee. This level of restriction may seem intense, but it's what makes the diet so effective.

2. Plan Your Meals Like a Pro

One of the biggest mistakes people make is not planning ahead. If you don't have meals ready, hunger can push you toward foods that aren't part of the diet. A good approach is to batch-cooking so there's always something available. Some meal ideas:

- Breakfast: A fatty ribeye steak—quick, satisfying, and packed with energy.

- Lunch: Lamb chops with a crispy sear, seasoned only with salt.

- Dinner: Slow-cooked goat stew, rich in collagen and nutrients.

We will have more practical meals later in this book.

Pro tip: If you feel sluggish at first, try eating more fat. The transition can be tough if your body isn't used to running on fat for fuel.

3. Choose High-Quality Meats (If Possible)

While any ruminant meat will work, grass-fed and grass-finished meats are ideal because they're higher in omega-3s and key nutrients. If you can't always get them, don't stress—just focus on fatty cuts like ribeye, brisket, or lamb shoulder to keep energy levels up.

4. Keep Cooking Simple

No need to overcomplicate things. Grill, roast, or slow-cook your meat, and let the natural flavors shine. If you're missing variety, experiment with different cuts—fattier meats will keep you fuller longer.

Once you get into a rhythm, the Lion Diet stops feeling restrictive and becomes effortless. The key is to be prepared and listen to your body's needs.

Tips for Transitioning Smoothly

Starting the Lion Diet can be a big shift, especially if you're used to a diet with more variety. Here are some ways to make the transition easier and set yourself up for success:

1. Ease Into It (If Needed)

If you're coming from a diet full of carbs and processed foods, cutting everything out overnight might be too much. Consider phasing out non-compliant foods over a week or two. Start by eliminating grains and sugar first, then move on to dairy and other non-ruminant meats before fully committing.

2. Stay on Top of Hydration

Drinking plenty of water is essential. Since this diet naturally lowers insulin, your body excretes more sodium and water, which can lead to dehydration or dizziness. Adding salt to your water helps maintain electrolyte balance and keeps energy levels stable.

3. Listen to Your Body

The first few days can feel rough—some people experience fatigue, digestive shifts, or cravings as their body adjusts.

This is normal. Take note of how you feel, increase your fat intake if you're low on energy, and rest when needed. Your body will adapt.

4. Find Support

This diet is restrictive, and going at it alone can feel isolating. Connecting with online communities or others who follow the Lion Diet can help you stay motivated, troubleshoot challenges, and share meal ideas. The Lion Diet community on Facebook can be very helpful.

1. Be Prepared for Cravings

Cravings are part of the process, especially if you're used to sugar, caffeine, or processed foods. When they hit, remind yourself why you started—better health, more energy, or relief from symptoms. Eating enough fat can also reduce cravings.

2. Navigate Social Situations

Eating out or attending gatherings can be tricky. If possible, eat beforehand or bring your own food. If dining out, steak or grilled lamb (without sauces) is usually a safe bet. It's okay to be upfront about your dietary needs—most people respect discipline.

3. Track Your Progress

Keeping a simple journal of your meals, symptoms, and energy levels can help you see patterns and improvements over time. Even small wins—like clearer skin, better digestion, or steady energy—can keep you motivated.

4. Check in with a Professional (If Needed)

The Lion Diet is extreme, and while many thrive on it, it's not for everyone. If you have underlying health conditions or concerns, working with a knowledgeable and open-minded healthcare provider can give you peace of mind and ensure you're on the right track.

Final Thought: The first couple of weeks are the hardest, stick with it, trust the process, and give your body time to adjust. You've got this!

Lion Diet Troubleshooting Guide: Common Challenges & Solutions

Transitioning to the Lion Diet can come with a few hurdles but understanding what to expect—and how to address it—can make the process much smoother.

1. Keto Flu & Electrolyte Imbalance

Symptoms: Fatigue, headaches, dizziness, muscle cramps, brain fog.

Solution:

- Drink salt water (mix ½ teaspoon of salt in a glass of water).

- Increase potassium and magnesium through mineral-rich salts or supplements.

- Stay hydrated—aim for at least 2–3 liters of water daily to prevent dehydration.

Why this happens: Your body is adjusting to lower insulin levels, causing it to flush out water and electrolytes. Replenishing them will help restore balance.

2. Digestive Issues (Constipation or Diarrhea)

Constipation:

- Eat fattier meat cuts like ribeye, brisket, or lamb to support digestion.

- Drink warm salt water or bone broth to stimulate bowel movements.

- Ensure adequate hydration throughout the day.

Diarrhea:

- Avoid consuming too much rendered fat (like drinking tallow).

- Stick to slow-cooked meat rather than fried or greasy options.

- Be patient, your gut needs time to adjust to a meat-only diet.

Why this happens: Your microbiome is adapting to a new way of eating, and your body may take a few weeks to regulate digestion.

3. Energy Dips & Weakness

Symptoms: Feeling sluggish, tired, or weak.

Solution:

- Eat more—many people underestimate how much they need.

- Focus on fatty meats to provide steady, long-lasting energy.

- Give your body time—fat adaptation takes 2–4 weeks.

Why this happens: Your body is shifting from burning carbohydrates to using fat as fuel, which takes time to fully transition.

4. Social Challenges & Cravings

Challenges: Eating out, peer pressure, or missing favorite foods.

Solution:

- Plan ahead—bring your own meals or choose restaurants that offer plain grilled meats.

- Keep your goals in mind—remind yourself why you started this journey.

- Join an online or local support community to stay motivated.

Why this happens: Social habits are deeply tied to food, but as you start feeling the benefits of this diet, the cravings and temptations often fade.

5. Mood Swings & Mental Adjustments

Symptoms: Irritability, anxiety, or emotional ups and downs.

Solution:

- Prioritize quality sleep (aim for 7–9 hours per night).

- Manage stress with light movement like walking or stretching.

- Ensure you're eating enough healthy fats to support brain function.

Why this happens: Dietary changes can influence neurotransmitters, but once stabilized, many reported improved mental clarity and emotional balance.

6. Nutrient Concerns & Long-Term Sustainability

Concern: Is this diet too restrictive?

Solution:

- The Lion Diet is not meant to be permanent for everyone—it's an elimination tool to help identify food sensitivities and reduce inflammation.

- Once stable, you can reintroduce low-inflammatory foods like eggs or seafood to expand your diet.

- Monitor your body's response and adjust as needed to ensure long-term sustainability.

Why this happens: The goal is not just restriction but healing and discovery—eventually finding the best diet for your unique needs.

Stage 0: Transitioning to the Lion Diet

- **Duration:** 1 to 4 weeks (depending on individual needs)

- **What to Eat:** Gradually reduce processed foods, grains, sugar, and high-inflammatory plant foods while increasing intake of animal-based foods like beef, lamb, and healthy fats.

- **Purpose:** To ease into the Lion Diet without extreme withdrawal symptoms, allowing the body to adapt gradually and minimizing potential side effects like fatigue or digestive discomfort.

Stage 1: Full Elimination (Strict Lion Diet)

- **Duration:** 2 to 8 weeks (or longer, depending on symptoms)

- **What to Eat:** Only ruminant meat (beef, lamb, goat, bison, etc.), salt, and water.

- **Purpose:** This phase removes all potential dietary irritants, allowing the body to heal from

inflammation, autoimmune reactions, and digestive
issues.

Stage 2: Stabilization & Monitoring

- **Duration:** Ongoing (can last several months)

- **What to Eat:** Continue strict Lion Diet until
symptoms fully stabilize.

- **Purpose:** This stage ensures that all health
improvements are maintained before reintroducing
any new foods. It helps determine if the diet alone is
resolving symptoms.

Stage 3: Careful Reintroduction (Optional)

- **Duration:** Gradual process (varies by individual)

- **What to Introduce:** Slowly add back one new food
at a time (e.g., eggs, dairy, fish, or low-inflammatory
plant foods like avocado) while monitoring
reactions.

- **Purpose:** To identify personal food tolerances and
determine which foods are safe to include without

triggering symptoms. Some people may choose to stay on the strict Lion Diet indefinitely.

Stage 4: Maintenance (Personalized Diet Plan)

- **Duration:** Long-term

- **What to Eat:** A customized diet based on tolerated foods. Some may expand to a broader carnivore diet, while others stick to Lion Diet principles.

- **Purpose:** To create a sustainable eating plan that maintains health improvement without unnecessary restrictions.

1. Pan-Seared Ribeye Steak

Ingredients: Ribeye steak, salt, water

Instructions:

Heat a cast-iron skillet on high.

Generously salt both sides of the steak.

Sear for 3-4 minutes per side until a crust forms.

Let it rest for 5 minutes before slicing.

2. Slow-Cooked Beef Short Ribs

Ingredients: Beef short ribs, salt, water

Instructions:

Preheat oven to 275°F (135°C).

Season ribs with salt and place in a roasting pan.

Add a small amount of water, cover with foil, and slow-cook for 3-4 hours until tender.

3. Bone Broth Soup

Ingredients: Beef bones, salt, water

Instructions:

Place bones in a large pot, cover with water, and add salt.

Simmer on low for 12-24 hours.

Strain and enjoy the rich broth.

4. Crispy Lamb Chops

Ingredients: Lamb chops, salt

Instructions:

Preheat a pan over medium-high heat.

Salt the chops and sear for 3-4 minutes per side.

Rest before serving.

5. Beef Tallow Roasted Brisket

Ingredients: Brisket, salt, beef tallow

Instructions:

Rub brisket with salt and cover with beef tallow.

Roast at 300°F (150°C) for 4-5 hours until fork-tender.

6. Lamb Shoulder Stew

Ingredients: Lamb shoulder, salt, water

Instructions:

Cut lamb into chunks and season with salt.

Simmer in water for 3-4 hours until tender.

7. Beef Fat Burgers (No Bun, No Seasoning)

Ingredients: Ground beef (80/20), salt

Instructions:

Form patties and season with salt.

Cook in a skillet for 3-4 minutes per side.

8. Reverse-Seared Tomahawk Steak

Ingredients: Tomahawk steak, salt

Instructions:

Cook at 250°F (120°C) for about 45 minutes.

Sear over high heat for 1-2 minutes per side.

9. Lamb Rib Rack

Ingredients: Lamb rack, salt

Instructions:

Salt the lamb and roast at 375°F (190°C) for 25-30 minutes.

Let it rest before slicing.

10. Beef Cheek Stew

Ingredients: Beef cheeks, salt, water

Instructions:

Slow-cook beef cheeks in salted water for 4-6 hours.

Shred and serve with broth.

11. Salted Beef Jerky

Ingredients: Thinly sliced beef, salt

Instructions:

Season meat with salt and dry in the oven at 175°F (80°C) for 4-6 hours.

12. Seared Lamb Liver

Ingredients: Lamb liver, salt

Instructions:

Slice liver and season with salt.

Sear in a hot pan for 1-2 minutes per side.

13. Boiled Oxtail Soup

Ingredients: Oxtail, salt, water

Instructions:

Simmer oxtail in salted water for 6-8 hours.

Enjoy the tender meat and rich broth.

14. Beef Belly Roast

Ingredients: Beef belly, salt

Instructions:

Salt the meat and roast at 325°F (160°C) for 3-4 hour.

4-Week Lion Diet Transition Plan

Goal: Reintroduce foods slowly & strategically while monitoring symptoms.

Method: Add one food every 3–5 days, increasing portions gradually.

Week 1&2: Expanding Animal-Based Foods

(Stick close to Lion Diet while testing additional animal-based options.)

•Egg yolks (start with yolks only; whites may cause reactions)

• Butter & ghee (best tolerated dairy fats)

• Duck fat & tallow (for added energy)

• Fatty fish (salmon, sardines, mackerel for omega-3s)

• Lamb & chicken (if tolerated well)

Monitor digestion, skin, and energy levels before moving forward.

Week 3&4: Testing Non-Ruminant Meats & Seafood

•Shellfish (shrimp, scallops, oysters) (high in nutrients, low risk)

•Turkey (pasture-raised) (leaner options for variety)

•More dairy testing: If butter was tolerated, try goat cheese or sheep's milk (easier to digest than cow dairy).

If you experience bloating, fatigue, or skin flare-ups, pause dairy.

Week 5&6: Introducing Low-Toxin Plant Foods (Only if you want plant-based food!)

•Olive oil & olives (healthy fats, anti-inflammatory)

•Avocados (low-carb, high in potassium)

•Coconut (oil, milk, or flakes) (great for energy)

If no issues arise, continue increasing portions gradually.

Week 7&8: Testing Low-Risk Carbs (If Needed for Energy)

•Raw honey (pure, unprocessed, good for energy)

•White rice (low in anti-nutrients, easy to digest)

• Well-cooked sweet potatoes (gentler on digestion than other carbs)

If you feel sluggish after adding carbs, return to animal-based eating.

Extra Tips for a Smooth Transition

✓ Eat one new food at a time to pinpoint problem foods.

✓ Prioritize nutrient-dense foods and avoid processed items.

✓ If a food causes issues, remove it and wait before testing another.

Grilled Wild Salmon

Ingredients: Wild-caught salmon fillet, salt

Instructions: Season the salmon with salt and grill until cooked through.

Honey-Glazed Chicken Thighs

Ingredients: chicken thighs, raw honey

Instructions: Brush chicken thighs with a thin layer of honey and bake until golden and cooked.

Pressure-Cooked Carrot and Parsnip Broth

Ingredients: Organic carrots, parsnips, water, salt

Instructions: Pressure cook chopped carrots and parsnips in water with a pinch of salt until tender. Strain and sip the broth.

Pan-Seared Fresh Tuna

Ingredients: Fresh tuna steak, salt

Instructions: Season the tuna with salt and sear in a hot pan to desired doneness.

Steamed Organic Pears

Ingredients: Organic pears, water

Instructions: Peel and slice pears, then steam until soft. Allow to cool before eating.

Baked Apples with Honey Drizzle

Ingredients: Organic apples, raw honey

Instructions: Core apples and bake until tender. Drizzle with a small amount of honey before serving.

Boiled Parsnips

Ingredients: Organic parsnips, water, salt

Instructions: Peel and chop parsnips, then boil in salted water until soft.

Honey-Sweetened Herbal Tea

Ingredients: Herbal tea (e.g., chamomile), raw honey

Instructions: Brew herbal tea and sweeten lightly with honey.

Grilled Mackerel

Ingredients: Wild mackerel fillets, salt

Instructions: Season fillets with salt and grill until cooked through.

Pressure-Cooked Organic Carrot Puree

Ingredients: Organic carrots, water, salt

Instructions: Pressure cook carrots until tender, then blend into a smooth puree.

MORE! MORE!! MORE!!!

Want our previous book on the lion diet with 30 meal plans? Want our free journal recipes?

Visit: bit.ly/4bbvU5R

We've Sold Over 200 Copies—But Need Your Help!

While over 200 copies have been sold, only 8 readers have left a rating, and 2 negative reviews have hurt the book's credibility and visibility. These buyers though it to be written by Jordan or Mikhaila Peterson, despite our clear disclaimer.

If you find value in this book, please take a minute to leave a review or rating. Your support helps others discover it and means a lot to the author. Just use the link or QR code—thank you!

If you enjoy the book, please consider leaving a review through this link.   - https://rb.gy/dmuolm or

by scanning this QR code: